KIND LEADERSHIP

How to make a difference

ABOUT THE AUTHOR

Neil Rothwell qualified as a clinical psychologist in 1981 and worked for 30 years in the National Health Service in Scotland. He has worked in the areas of mental health and brain injury. In the second half of his career he was in clinical management positions. This included running a national brain injury rehabilitation service with forty staff, and also managing a service providing therapy for people referred by their family doctor with problems such as recurrent depression and severe anxiety.

He is now working freelance, including training staff in mindfulness-based therapies.

CONTENTS

Introduction

1. Why Are You Doing This?

The importance of you as an individual and what motivates you.

2. Space and Decision-making

Effective decision-making requires adequate reflection. This chapter describes how to do this.

3. Giving People the Opportunity to be Involved

How to make your staff the heart of the organisation.

4. People as the Key Resource

The staff are the people who actually produce the work. How to draw on the strength of each individual.

5. Create Conversations

Connecting with relevant people creates new ways of taking things forward.

6. Ownership

Positive and sustainable change will happen when staff team members are an active part of the planning and implementation process.

7. Letting Go of Control

Sometimes, allowing yourself to be lost can enable a learning cycle to take place.

8. Be a Catalyst

How everything a leader does can inspire change.

9. Taking Responsibility

Letting go of control still means making difficult decisions sometimes and helping staff with their concerns.

10. The Role of Strategy

A quick and effective way to find direction and start moving forward.

11. An Example

A description of how change happened in the author's work.

12. Not a Leader?

Ways of positively influencing the system when you are not the one in power.

13. Leadership and Kindness

Why kindness produces positive change.

References

Introduction

This book is aimed at people who have significant responsibility at work or in another area of their life, especially those who lead or influence others in some capacity. Perhaps you have recently been promoted or obtained a new post at a higher level of challenge than previously. Or maybe you have been in a managerial position for many years and feel demotivated or stressed out. Perhaps you are working well already and simply open to new ideas. You may be a caring professional whose responsibility includes clients or patients as well as other staff. The purpose of this book is to help you perform these roles effectively by showing that the best outcomes are obtained by starting with the people who are doing the work - your staff, other people you work with – and yourself. Outcomes, profits and success have no existence independent of the people who are producing them. Much management guidance takes outcomes and goals as the starting point and, of course, it is important to have some sense of direction and purpose. What this can translate into, however, is a leader identifying their goals and then trying to enable (or make) their staff to follow these. This is usually not the most effective way of working because it creates a number of unnecessary difficulties. Instead, by centring the outcomes around the people who do the work, everyone makes the results happen rather than just one person - the leader. Put like this, it may seem obvious, but in practice many leaders behave in an unnecessarily authoritarian way.

What I will be describing is relatively simple to understand. Many management and leadership texts use quite complicated models. This can make it easy to become lost in the detail of the approach, whereas, one of the key features of leadership is being able to cut through detail to see the bigger picture. It can be tempting to take refuge in complex frameworks in order to avoid having to make difficult decisions. While the approach described here is simple in principle, it is not necessarily straightforward to implement.

It would be nice to be able to say that there is a fixed blueprint which, if followed, would give guaranteed results. Leadership is more subtle than that and it is important to be able to let go of the need to control outcomes and people. Instead, this approach offers a clear set of guidelines, grounded in the real world, which has been shown to be effective in a wide range of work situations.

I will be using the term "leadership" throughout the book. It is a clear and simple term which everyone understands. It is different from management even though many managers do have a leadership role. "Management" often includes a range of technical and operational roles which are about maintaining existing quality rather than promoting positive change. On the other hand, "leadership" can be misleading in some ways. It suggests a person who stands above others and focuses on that person as the driver of change. Instead, this book will see the leader as someone who stands alongside other staff and supports them, whilst still taking responsibility overall. It also proposes that leadership is a fluid role that can be taken by different people as the situation demands, or shared between more than one person. This also highlights that anyone in an organisation can take what is in effect a leadership role in terms of promoting change and inspiring others. I therefore hope this book will be of interest to you whether or not you have a formal leadership role. Chapter 12 focuses specifically on making changes if you do not have a leadership role, and for the rest of the book, assume the word "leader" applies to you!

Work is a major part of most people's lives, yet it for many it is a source of difficulty. In 2017/18, 595,000 people suffered from work-related stress in the UK, resulting in 15.4 million lost working days [1]. In 2007 this condition cost Great Britain over £530 million. Gallup has estimated that actively disengaged employees cost the US economy $370 billion and Singapore $4.9 billion each year. Employee engagement is defined as an emotional commitment to one's employer and feeling motivated by the organisation's leaders.

Although money is a major reason for working, money in itself doesn't make the work enjoyable or productive. People can be profoundly unhappy at their work whilst earning a good salary. There are other factors that are at least as significant. Perhaps the most important of these is self-respect. Work is a major part of how people identify themselves. All jobs are valuable in some way. Most people know this and, given the opportunity, want to perform to the best of their ability. To do this, they need to be able to express themselves in their work. Performing a job like a machine is a recipe for demoralisation. Similarly, they want to be creative. There are different ways of doing even the most mundane job and these ways change as the situation changes and the person learns more. Also, work is a contribution to society and we want to feel that our contribution is valuable. Being part of a bigger undertaking is an important function of work. Unfortunately many workplaces do not provide these opportunities.

In writing this book, I am drawing on 30 years of working in the National Health Service in the UK as a clinical psychologist. Half of this time was as a service manager. The NHS is a complex environment where decision-making is involves many stakeholders. Funding does not usually follow productivity but is the result of political decisions, yet there is a constant pressure to increase productivity in order to meet patient needs and reduce waiting times. I found it was possible to improve services significantly without relying on increased funding and staffing, and the approach outlined here is based on this. In Chapter 11, I describe some of this work and its outcomes. I have also been involved in a leadership role with a number of charitable (non-profit) organisations in different settings. In all this work I have learned that the most effective change is made, not by trying to make it happen, but by helping others to work successfully and fulfil a collective vision. Similar principles have been used in the industrial and commercial sectors with impressive results [2].

Chapter 1

Why Are You Doing This?

This question relates to your reasons for working. It may seem a strange place to start a book on leadership, but I believe that it points to the heart of what it means to be an effective leader. Our attitudes affect the way we behave, which in turn determines how effective we are.

Perhaps the most obvious reason for being a leader is money. It has been suggested that money is what we are given for the use of our life energy at work [3]. Leaders tend to be paid well. This makes sense, as having responsibility is generally not easy and takes energy to do. Money is important, both to fulfil our needs and to pay for the enjoyments in life. Even so, research has shown that levels of pay have only a small influence on job satisfaction [4]. Money is undoubtedly a motivator but it is generally not the only reason why people work.

What about ambition? The dictionary defines this as "aspiration after success" [5]. We obtain a leadership role as a recognition of our abilities and achievements, and this is clearly satisfying. We want to succeed further and this gives us motivation, which is necessary to achieve anything. Making changes in an organisation takes time and effort. So ambition can be useful in this respect. Yet taken to excess, it can have a negative side. It may cause us to act disrespectfully to other employees in order to "get ahead" of them or achieve results at any cost.

Another possible motivating factor is power. Definition: "the ability to do anything...capacity for producing an effect". Looked at this way, power is essential in order to make any useful changes. The ability to make decisions regarding others is a defining feature of power e.g. the ability to "hire and fire". Power is a complex issue that has been much studied, often in a way that seems to imply that it is a destructive force. Certainly, we don't need to look far in the modern world to see problems caused by the abuse of power. In work situations, too, power can be transformed into bullying in the wrong hands. This is combining power with the use of fear as a way of controlling people. But it is possible to use power in a benign way, without combining it with manipulation. When we talk about "influence" we are pointing to this possibility.

One of the reasons you may have for wanting to earn a good income is to provide for family or others. There is a degree of altruism in this. We can be doing our work for the benefit of others in some way, even for the benefit of society as a whole. This motivation is clear in workers in caring organisations but can be present in many situations. Business can produce economic growth, which can benefit society generally. This points to another reason for taking a leadership post – to develop a sense of purpose in life. Even the most unfulfilling job can provide this, whether it is contributing to the common good or providing an income to improve the quality of your life. There are many people who perform work for nothing. Some of them are working for charitable or community organisations. Others are parenting a child or caring for a sick relative (or both). Another category of people are earning less than their abilities would allow them in order to pursue work that is meaningful for them. All of these are motivated by having a sense of fulfilment in what they are doing. If you asked them, they may not put in in that way, but the very act of doing it day after day, week after week, attests to this.

Yet even these altruistic motives can have a negative side. The intention is to improve the world in some way. This is excellent in itself, but sometimes it can come from an inflexible attitude, perhaps based in desperation at the state of the world. The action that arises from this attitude can often have a hard edge to it. For example, bullying does sometimes occur in caring organisations. It is as if the leader regards the outcome as so important that it justifies causing distress to their team members. There is an irony in how an attempt to create a caring environment can have uncaring side effects. We sometimes see similar problems in the field of political action, where the desire for a better society can lead to unhelpful - or even violent – results. More generally, this illustrates the impossibility of separating results from the process of attaining them.

How is all this relevant to leadership? The main tool you have as a leader is yourself as an individual. What comes across to others most strongly, be they employees, bosses, colleagues, clients, is how you are. Humans have a great sensitivity to each other and can detect the most subtle behaviours. We unconsciously watch each other, picking up on non-verbal cues, noticing the response of others. To lead and influence, you need the trust and respect of others. Yes, it is possible to use authority to make people do things, and this can work in the short-term. But the progress made in this way tends to be brittle; it is essentially using fear as a motivator. Sooner or later the workforce become demoralised, resentful and performance decreases. Increasing amounts of resources and energy become used up in monitoring the workforce, trying to motivate them and filling posts of people who are off work with stress.

Much of the way we come across to others is based on our intentions. Are we doing things in the best interests of all – including the people we are working with – or are we primarily motivated by ensuring our own personal success? These are the signals we will be sending out to staff and will affect how sincere they perceive us to be and therefore how much to trust us. A lot of this will be at an unconscious or non-verbal level, which can be at least as important as conscious communication.

By reflecting on your motives you become more honest with yourself and this naturally causes others to see you as more trustworthy. None of the reasons given above for leading (money, power, ambition, altruism) are a problem in themselves, it is more about how we use them. Seeing ourselves more clearly gives us a choice of how we use these, either for our own gratification or the benefit of all. In practice, we are all a mixture of motivations, positive and negative, and we do not have to be perfect in order to lead effectively. This means you can look at yourself in a relaxed and gentle way. Simply asking "why am I doing this?" and seeing what you notice is enough. You may not get a neat answer but that is OK – the very act of asking demonstrates an openness and sincerity. And you don't have to do this all the time - just checking in with yourself from time-to-time is enough.

It is also worth bearing in mind that "the best interests of all" includes yourself. We are not separate from the situation we find ourselves in, so we can take our own needs into account. By looking carefully, it is usually possible to find a position that works for both ourselves and our staff, customers, patients etc. Again, this does not require perfection. A genuine attempt to do the best we can is the most effective way to make a positive difference.

Putting it into Practice – What Are my Motivations?

This is a short exercise to help you reflect on your reasons for working. There are no right or wrong answers – simply answer as honestly as you can, then think about what you have written and how it affects your work.

Rate each of the statements below using the following scale:

1   2   3   4   5   6   7   8   9   10

Strongly   Neither agree   Strongly
disagree   nor disagree   agree

Use your score as a basis for reflecting on your motivation in this area.

*I am heavily motivated by **money***

*I am heavily motivated by **power***

*I am heavily motivated by **ambition***

*I am heavily motivated by **altruism**.*

Chapter 2

Space and Decision-making

I was once given extra responsibility in a job, which involved me spending time in a workplace I hadn't been before. After meeting people I found myself having a couple of days with absolutely nothing to do. I set up my office, washed the windows, then started having a look around. It was a psychological therapy service with a very long waiting list. There were around 180 patients on this list, many of whom had already been waiting a long time for individual therapy. At that time, virtually everyone referred to the service would be offered one-to-one therapy, irrespective of their problems. With the free time on my hands, I started looking through the list. I had previously been involved in running large-scale therapy courses and found about 80 people who seemed to be suitable for this rather than needing individual therapy. We were able to find a small amount of funding to employ staff to assess these people and run courses for them. Most patients took up the offer of the course and were able to receive appropriate treatment much quicker than they otherwise would have done. This saved some 35 weeks of therapist time (which would have been used on individual therapy that wasn't really needed) and reduced the waiting list by 40%. Quite a pay-off for two days of having nothing to do! This brought home to me the importance of having space as a leader. Given the choice, I would have found other things to keep myself busy and perhaps lost the opportunity presented by this space.

Most of us have had to work hard to reach the position we are in. School exams, qualifications, rising through the job ranks, starting a business – success is usually hard won. Many cultures also stress the importance of hard work, the implications being that long hours are essential for success and "more is better". This may be true for certain earlier parts of our career but as we get more responsibility, the ability to make decisions becomes more important, and the implications of those decisions can have far-reaching effects. This requires time to think and reflect. It can be difficult to let go of the idea that in order to do an effective job you have to be hyper-active and look busy, but this tends to lead to decisions of the knee-jerk variety, ones that are not sufficiently thought through. It is less about working hard and more about working smart. This is especially true in times of economic downturn where "more of the same" easily leads to increased workloads and staff burn-out. We need to be able to think differently and creatively. This is one of the key roles of leadership. The ideas may come from the leader or it may be team members who suggests them. Either way, they require time and careful consideration.

It is worth reflecting on what goes into making a decision. Broadly speaking, there are two phases to this. The first is understanding. We work in complex environments and finding out in detail what is actually going on is no small undertaking. Spending time with team members, colleagues, customers and anyone else involved is essential to this. Gathering information and data is also usually important. We then have a combination of hard and soft data, both of which are typically required. The second phase is deciding how to move forward on the basis of this understanding. It can be helpful to have some way of laying out the issues. My own preference is Mind Maps [6] but there are many programmes and apps that can help, or a flipchart or piece of paper can suffice. Whatever you use, it should help clarify your thinking. If it just adds another layer of complexity, use something else. Gathering information in this way is only a means to an end. Understanding can never be perfect, and at some point it is necessary to move to the next phase, which is making a decision.

Creating thinking time and space is important for both phases. In the information gathering phase, it is necessary to think about who to talk to and what information to gather. When talking to people, it is helpful to give them the space to air their views. People need time to relax into a conversation and often the more informal the chat, the more open the person is and the more valuable the insights gained. Some space for reflection is also needed when looking at data and information in order to determine what is important and what isn't.

The second phase of decision-making is, of course, crucial yet it is not easy to describe in detail. It is essential to have as deep an understanding as possible from the phase of information gathering and consideration, but then the actual decision relies heavily on a sense of intuition as to what feels right in the circumstances. It may well be helpful to weigh up the pros and cons, do option appraisals and projections and rely on your experience and that of the team but none of these actually make the decision. Ultimately, this relies on your sense of what feels right. Your intuition has implicitly been recognised by the fact that you are now in a position of leadership or responsibility, so it is a valuable asset. To work effectively, the intuition again requires space in which to operate. It is a process which largely goes on in our unconscious mind. The unconscious is a wonderful resource which processes information and ideas outside our awareness and then can present them to our conscious mind. In order for this to happen, space is needed for the unconscious ideas to "bubble up" in our minds. The promptings are often subtle and we need to listen to ourselves and the situation to hear them.

The effects of doing this can be huge. Many people have had life changing experiences both at work and in their personal lives by listening to their hunches [7]. On the other hand, one of the main reason that things go wrong is that some aspect of a situation has been overlooked. This can happen because decision-makers focus so much on what they want to happen, rather than the realities of the situation, that they do not listen to their intuition. So, far from being a waste of time, taking space to listen and understand is usually the most efficient way of achieving results.

Decisions can be big or small. Much of your day-to-day work probably involves "micro-decisions" which do not require profound thought. Nonetheless, it is helpful to take a moment's pause for reflection. Sometimes small decisions end up having significant implications, or a series of small actions adds up to a major sea change. Any time invested in this process is well rewarded. Not infrequently, I am asked about something and am not sure whether it is a good idea or not. In these situations it is helpful to take a bit of time to think about it and get back to the person. Having time to let it sink in, things can occur to me that I would have missed if I had made the decision immediately. The temptation is to agree to a request straight away in order to keep the person happy. If the request seems straightforward, it is nice to be able to agree to it. But if I notice a nagging sense of doubt in my mind, experience has told me that it is best to give myself space to think, and perhaps find more out about the situation. Many staff who come to you will understand this need to think about an issue and they will probably appreciate the fact that you are taking the request seriously.

Another feature of decisions is that they are subject to change. Circumstances change and what is a good course of action at one point may need modifying at another. This is another reason to keep "listening" to your own sense of the situation. Flexibility is a key attribute of an effective leader. This isn't the same as being indecisive. It may be that what you sense is the need to just keep going in a particular direction even when some voices are criticising that direction. A balance is needed between trusting your intuition and checking in with others. It is very helpful to have a supportive figure you can check out your ideas with. This may be a boss, one of your team or someone outside your immediate work situation. The important thing is that you can talk openly to them and can trust them, both in terms of their views and their ability to maintain confidentiality. You may or may not decide to take their advice. I have often found that just being able to talk to someone who is willing to listen helps me to clarify my own thinking. There is a psychological principle which says: "as I hear myself talk, I learn what I believe", and talking through issues enables this to happen.

How to Find Space

- *Decide to take time out, say an afternoon.*

- *If need be, clear it with your boss and explain the benefit to the organisation of what you are doing.*

- *Find somewhere away from your workplace where you won't be interrupted. Going for a walk or to a cafe can be helpful.*

- *You may feel there are many reasons you should not be doing this. Notice these but don't act on them.*

- *During the time out, think about your work, where it's going, and any issues related to it.*

- *Let your mind wander freely – this is partly about being creative and seeing things in a new light.*

- *Write things down if you want.*

- *You can also do this by talking it through with a colleague.*

- *A few days later, think back on that time and decide if it was time well spent.*

Chapter 3

Giving People the Opportunity to be Involved

This book is really about people, so let's take a closer look at them. Your most important group are your team. These are the people who you either directly manage or whose work you oversee in some way. As a leader you are dependent on them as they are the ones actually doing most of the work. Each one is an individual, and we could look at their motivations in the same way as we did with you in Chapter 1. Each of them is there for a reason i.e. they are motivated in some way. Most staff want to do their job well. We all want to be able to respect ourselves, and being a good worker is part of this. For this reason, we can have a basic trust in the workforce. A key role of leadership then becomes how to provide the conditions to enable the workforce to do their job as well as possible.

The psychologist Carl Rogers had some interesting things to say about this in his person-centred theory of human development [8]. He used an agricultural metaphor. When growing plants, what is needed is to provide the right conditions of water, soil and sunshine. A plant has a built-in ability to grow and develop and will do this automatically given these conditions. No other input is required. He applied this analogy to people. People also have a self-drive to succeed and will do so if we give them the right conditions. The conditions he identified are warmth, genuineness and empathy. The more one person displays these qualities to another person, the better that other person will tend to perform. This is a general theory that applies to a wide range of settings e.g. schools, therapy services – and workplaces. Let's look at these conditions more closely.

Warmth is the emotional warmth we feel, for example, to someone we like. A more technical term Rogers used was unconditional positive regard. "Unconditional" means seeking to have respect for them irrespective of whether or not we like them. It entails a recognition of their ability to develop as individuals, their desire to do the best they can and to learn from their mistakes. It does not stand against giving advice or direction. In fact the person is more likely to listen to the advice if they feel that you are doing in a supportive and respectful way, even if it is hard to hear. More commonly, though, it is about recognising the positive contribution they are making and drawing attention to this. It is very easy to take things for granted and this applies to the work that people do day after day. A word of encouragement from an influential person (like yourself) can do wonders for someone's motivation.

Genuineness is something we can easily recognise in others. It is a sense of honesty, a lack of hidden agendas, being straightforward rather than hiding behind a role. It is sometimes called congruence, meaning that what someone is saying matches the non-verbal messages they are communicating. Being genuine is about being honest with yourself, open to your feelings and being non-judgemental towards yourself. It is normal to have an emotional response to many situations at work. If you are feeling emotional, it is best to acknowledge this, otherwise you may be acting on a passing feeling rather than what's really best in a situation. For a moment, focussing on yourself, rather than the external situation, can be helpful. You can label the emotion e.g. saying to yourself "I am feeling angry right now". Just acknowledging your feelings in this way means that they no longer have the same power over you. It is not necessary to try and get rid of the feeling – it will fade itself naturally over time, though not necessarily straight away. There is no need to criticise yourself for your feelings – it simply proves you are alive! We can think of it as warmth towards ourselves, recognising that we, too, are trying to do the best we can. If we take this self-respecting inward attitude, we will naturally come across as genuine. It have does not mean we have to say everything we feel (which can be insensitive). Genuineness is as much about how you *are* as what you say.

Empathy involves seeing the world through another person's eyes. People have a built-in empathy for each other. This is what makes television and film dramas so compulsive – we can identify with the actors' feelings even though we know at another level that it's not real. Being on the receiving end of empathy is a powerful experience. To feel understood is to feel cared about, and this is both empowering and lifts morale. As a leader, understanding what is important to your team members and colleagues means that they will feel committed both to you and the work you are all doing. Empathy shows itself by the way we relate to someone. It might be simply asking "how are you?" or taking time to listen to someone's concerns about their work.

These are qualities you can develop within yourself over time. The first step is to recognise them as important. It is easy to dismiss these qualities as just being "nice", and naïve in the hard-nosed world of work. In fact, being nice in itself can improve business performance [9]. Also, simply having these qualities in mind when talking to people can make a difference. Typically, when we try to be person-centred, one thing we notice is when we fail to be so. You may feel cold towards someone, or be so preoccupied with your agenda that you do not listen to their concerns. Seeing these difficulties is actually very useful. Once we see something, we can then start to change it, a process that is sometimes called "experiential learning". We have a natural ability to develop in terms of recognising what works and learning from our mistakes.

The person-centred approach has sometimes been called "non-directive" but this is a misunderstanding. In his early work, Rogers used this term but he soon abandoned it, focusing instead on the above conditions for a successful relationship. It is quite possible to combine being person-centred with having a strategic vision. We can also give someone instructions, or be firm with them, in a way that is warm, genuine and empathic. The person will be able to receive this much better if we are expressing these qualities. So this does not stand against being strong and assertive.

The message is that being supportive and real with your staff will increase their motivation and performance. It is worth spending a moment to reflect on what motivation is. Consider someone who sits around all day watching television. Are they unmotivated? At one level, of course they are. Yet we could also say they are very motivated - to sit around! This is not a trivial point. People are always making choices and do everything for a reason, even if they are not conscious of it. People might sit around because they feel safe in the house, or because watching TV distracts them from worries, or because they are so lacking in energy it is all they feel capable of doing. So motivation is always there, it is simply the direction of the motivation that is the issue. If you see a worker as being unmotivated, it is helpful to see their motivation as simply going in a different direct from what you would like it to. You want them to perform well but they have some other motivation. By being person-centred with them, it is possible to find out what this is and help them get on board with the work. Even if they are performing well, they may have motivations that you don't know about and could be useful to the organisation.

There have been times in my own work when I have put in large amounts of energy into a project with little effect. These were times when I was unable to tap into the motivation of the people I was working with. At other times, the results from a relatively small amount of input have been striking. I had an experience of this when I worked with people just outside Edinburgh whose mental health difficulties meant that they had to have long-term contact with psychiatric services, sometimes including long spells as hospital in-patients. Traditionally, this group of people were passive recipients of the service, being subject to treatment decisions from the expert health professionals. They were also regarded as a generally "unmotivated" group. Around this time, there was the beginning of interest in patients having more say in the organisation of mental health services. I ended up inviting a service user from England who had been involved in starting a user-led advocacy service, to give a talk to local patients. The response was astonishing. A large number of local service users came to the talk and many were keen to start something locally, despite struggling themselves with mental health problems. This led to the start of a user-led project which is still operating over 20 years later. It seemed that I had, so to speak, opened a door - a possibility - and then a whole lot of energy from people flowed in through this. This had tapped into their motivation, or passion – to have more control over their lives.

It can be tempting, in a busy job, to regard spending a lot of time trying to motivate staff as an optional extra and not the top priority. People are getting paid to do the work, so why not just give them clear instructions and expect them to get on with it? This is true at one level and works quite well in many situations. However, it does have limitations. In any case, I am not suggesting you try and "motivate staff" - motivation is not something we can give to someone else. It is more about tapping into their passion, releasing their own motivation. Then they are likely to do an excellent rather than an OK job. If they feel they are being listened to and respected, they will also tend to be more creative, for example finding better ways to do the work than you, or they, had previously thought of, or coming up with completely new ideas.

The same principle applies to the other groups of people you work with: colleagues, clients, students, audience, people in other organisations. It is an effective way of dealing with conflict and misunderstandings. There is an old Indian story about a group of blind men touching an elephant to see what shape it was. One felt the leg and said "an elephant is like a column", another felt the trunk and said, "that's wrong, an elephant is like a flexible pipe". A third felt the elephant's side and said "you're both mistaken, an elephant is like a wall". They were all right in one way but they each had only a part of the picture. By being empathic and listening to the other person in a conflict, you can understand their position better and gain a larger perspective of the situation. Quite often, when the other person sees you trying to understand them, they will soften their own position, making an agreement more likely.

The same is also true of your own boss. It is common to see those who make decisions affecting us, especially our boss, as somehow different from ourselves. Yet they are still human beings trying to make sense of the world. You may find that taking the approach above improves your relationship with them. This is not to say that bosses don't sometimes abuse power and, if this is the case, it needs to be recognised and appropriate action taken. Even in this case, the outcome is likely to be better if the above questions are considered.

Becoming Person-Centred

Ask yourself the following questions about groups of people you work with. You can do this for people individually and/or consider the group as a whole:

- *What is the quality of my relationship with them?*
- *How am I with them?*
- *Do I listen to them?*
- *Do I understand their passions and concerns?*
- *How warm do I feel towards them?*
- *Am I real with them or do I try to put on a front?*
- *Do I understand how they see things?*

Chapter 4

People as the Key Resource

We tend to think of our work in terms of output but really our work only has meaning because of other people. If you are making a product, it is a product that other people want. If it is a service, it's one that people need or want. And whatever your output, it will be produced by other people as well as yourself. Even a single person making things needs suppliers of raw materials and customers. So really, work is all about relationships. If you have a team that functions well, everything else will follow more smoothly. The question is, how to make the team run well.

Human beings are quite amazing when looked at objectively. The complexity of the body, let alone the brain, is staggering. Our ability to learn, adapt and create seems limitless, and we have striking abilities to cope with adversity, solve difficult problems, commit to a project, see it through to a conclusion and endure times of tedium. Every person who works with you has these qualities. We often tend to focus on a person's difficulties, on the assumption that addressing these will improve the situation. It might, but the real foundation of effective support is a deep appreciation of their abilities. If we look for problems, we will only see problems.

It is quite revealing to recognise the strengths of each person you work with. The exercise at the end of this chapter will help you with this. Like any habit of mind, it becomes easier the more you do it. Once you start thinking in this way, you may find your view of the work environment changes. Instead of a set of problems, what may reveal itself is a set of solutions based on team members playing to their strengths.

This can have implications for the type of work a person does. It is important that workers feel able to express themselves in their work. Is what they are doing capitalising on their strengths? This does not relate only to creativity. Some people are good at sustaining steady work over a long period of time, and feel happiest doing this. Others will thrive on change. In order to optimise the "fit" of the person to the work, some changes may be helpful. It may be that they can do their work in a different way that increases their engagement. Alternatively, it may be good for them to change jobs. This is best done in collaboration with the person themselves. In general, the more people feel they are doing the job they want, the better they will perform. At the same time, people do not always recognise their own strengths. Often they are self-critical, having a limited view of their abilities, and you may be able to see things in them that they do not recognise. Occasionally, they may think that they are good at something you feel they are not so good at. This requires sensitivity. It is likely that you will have recognised other strengths they have, and drawing attention to this will help ease the conversation and point to new possibilities.

This approach also has implications for relating to your team and others day by day. I would suggest that the default position for a conversation is appreciation. This can be expressed in many ways. Perhaps the most common is your general manner. Making friendly eye contact, listening, being alert and bright – these non-verbal behaviours can make an enormous difference. Have you ever gone to a doctor and found they didn't really listen, talked over you, were patronising or looked bored? If so, you probably came away feeling frustrated or demoralised. On the other hand, if the doctor listened carefully, looked attentive and took your views on board you are likely to have feel relieved and energised after. In both cases, the consultation may have been 10 minutes or less yet the effect was radically different. This is an illustration the significant effect an influential person can have on us even in a short time frame. I once read in an Italian phrase book how Italians tend not to say "please" and "thank you" as much as British or American people, yet still transmit these by their tone of voice – another example of non-verbal behaviour. Psychologists are still debating the amount how much communication is non-verbal. In everyday situations, it may not be as high as the 93% widely quoted – but they are all agreed that non-verbal behaviour is very important.

In terms of verbal feedback, expressing thanks is a powerful form of appreciation. As we take a more appreciative stance and realise the positive element of a person's contribution, it is natural that we will feel more grateful for what they are doing. This can be done in a quite ordinary and straightforward way. A simple "thanks" often works. Praise can also be helpful. It is particularly effective when specific e.g. "the careful way you listened to that customer really helped them feel comfortable and contributed to them making a purchase". At other times, a simple "nice job" can be appropriate. It is possible to use praise excessively, and then it starts to lose its meaning. Staff also need to be primarily self-motivated, as we have discussed, rather than dependent on praise. Non-verbal respect and simple gratitude can – and should - be used routinely.

It almost goes without saying that all this feedback should be genuine. Any increase in productivity is best seen as a side effect rather than the main reason for doing it. If you take an appreciative stance, it will be genuine. It will come out of your real inner feelings rather than being a superficial veneer. Nonetheless, giving expression to your appreciation is to some extent a skill which can benefit from practice. It also may feel awkward to begin if you are not used to doing it, or start trying it a different way. This is OK. We all have an acute ability to sense what someone really feels, so the person you are talking to will see through any awkwardness.

I am not suggesting here that you need to be always overflowing with goodwill. None of us feel like that a lot of the time, and fortunately we don't have to. Just having the intention and willingness to take this approach is what matters. For all of us, it is an ongoing learning process. As I said in chapter 3, genuineness includes our negative feelings as well as positive ones – we take a non-judgemental stance to both. One common source of frustration comes from feeling that a team member is not doing a job as well as you could. This is quite likely, as you have reached your position as a result of skill gained through experience, and the team member may still be learning some of these skills. Learning is one of the aspects of a job that makes it fulfilling, so it is important that all team members have the right to make mistakes – and to learn from them. It may be true that, if everyone in the team had your level of skill, things might go better. But then they would have to be employed at your grade as well!

The administration department of any organisation is often very busy and in a health service it is particularly so. Admin staff need to be highly organised to be maximally effective. A few years ago I found myself becoming frustrated with one the admin staff in our department (although fortunately I kept this frustration largely to myself). He seemed to me rather disorganised and not always reliable in what he did. Even so, he was always good-natured and willing to do the work given to him. A short while later, a colleague of mine was starting a new project and, to my surprise, she recruited this staff member to a job that involved a lot of networking and developing information systems. He flourished in this job, developed new skills and was much happier. In my frustration, I had only seen the difficulties the staff member had in his present job, whereas my colleague had been able to recognise other strengths which made him an ideal candidate for the new post. Looking with an appreciative eye can be like taking off a pair of dark glasses which has been limiting our vision.

Recognising Team Members' Strengths

Write down the names your key people, and against each of their names list their unique strengths, abilities and positive personal characteristics. It does not need to be a long list – a small number of points for each person will suffice. If it seems difficult at first, this may be a sign that you are not used to thinking in this way. Give yourself time to think about it.

Chapter 5

Create Conversations

I once went to a conference of community organisations in Glasgow. One of the speakers used the phrase "create conversations" to describe how he developed new initiatives and joint working. It was a phrase that stayed with me. I have been in organisations where lack of interactive working has been a major stumbling block to moving the organisation forward. In one, I was a member of one of three services that were doing very similar work. They had developed independently, from different professional backgrounds, and there was competitiveness and suspicion between them which inhibited co-operation. Closer working between the three would have been to everybody's advantage but it was difficult to make this happen. After a situation where our department came off worse in an unnecessarily competitive situation, I decided the only way forward was to create conversations with the other two services. There had been joint meetings before without much progress but it felt important to try again. I suggested a simple service development within an area which was fairly unthreatening and which gave a focus to the discussions. Over time, the services were able to build up more mutual trust and the development was implemented.

We are social creatures and the popularity of meetings and gatherings attests to the usefulness of getting together. Certainly, meetings can become so formal they lose any sense of dynamism and just feel like a ritual but even these can have useful spin-offs. The very act of getting together creates connections between people that may bear fruit in other ways. There have been many times I have decided to contact someone about an issue because I met them at an otherwise boring meeting.

The key word here is "create". Creating conversations is about taking an initiative. It might be as simple as turning to the person next to you or as complex as organising an international conference. When people start talking, things tend to start happening. Steve Jobs recognised this when he arranged for most of the staff at Pixar to be in a central area in their new offices. He knew that this would lead to more interaction between staff and better creativity [10]. One of the key roles of a leader is to make things happen and this usually requires having a conversation or discussion. This is especially so as we are aiming to create the conditions for things to happen rather than forcing anything. Making progress is a collaborative process, and the best ideas might not come forward from yourself as leader. What you will have done, though, is take the initiative in looking at the situation and talking about it.

Creating conversations often involves crossing boundaries (or, to use the popular management term, "silos") and this can, in itself be significant. It is reaching out to another person or group. One of the important effects of this is to build trust. Trust has many beneficial effects. It allows sharing to take place and unblocks the flow of information. It allows both parties to relax more, and in relaxing thinking becomes clearer and we become more open to new opportunities [11]. It may lead to joint working, maximising the strengths of the individual groups. On the surface, trust might seem to go against the competitive principle that seems to drive business but this is not necessarily the case. One successful advertising agency in the U.S. has flourished by helping its competitors [12].

One of the features of trust is that it can take time to build, especially where there has been mistrust. I left my post shortly after the example I gave at the start of this chapter and I felt that, in some ways, the work had only just begun. Trust-building is often an ongoing process which requires some patience. A discussion might seem to go nowhere fast but after it you may realise that something useful has, or can be, changed, or maybe the next time you meet things will go smoother because you know each other a little better. We all have an inbuilt drive to build connections with others and meeting together is an expression of this.

There are basically two ways of starting a conversation. One is to simply put yourself in the way of someone and start chatting. This is especially good for getting to know someone new in a situation where you both happen to be, for example, a conference. It is surprising how often something interesting or useful comes out of these conversations. Some people do this more naturally than others. I have to admit that I was not a natural at this and I have found it helpful to make a deliberate effort to make connections with people in this way. Like any skill, it becomes easier with practice and there are books that can help [13]. The other way of creating contact is by having a focus. It may be a proposal or request for information. It is probably better if it is something with potential benefit for the other person as well as yourself. This can make it easier to approach someone you would not otherwise meet e.g. by email or phone. Of course, you will have a genuine reason for wanting to meet them in the first place, so it is often not necessary to have a pretext. As a mentor of mine used to say, "if in doubt, tell the truth". A focus is also helpful if there is a degree of mistrust between you. If the agenda is one that the other person (or people) agrees with, it will immediately help relax things between you.

For creating a conversation with someone you already know, it can be helpful to look at them with a fresh pair of eyes. In Zen, this is called "beginner's mind". The Zen teacher Shunryu Suzuki said, "in the beginner's mind there are many possibilities, but in the expert's there are few" [14]. We carry in our minds a whole set of expectations about someone we know, based on our experience with them. If we focus too much on these, they can become a self-fulfilling prophecy – we see only what we are looking for and unconsciously filter out behaviour that does not fit with this. This is why Suzuki says that the expert's mind can be limited. People can change, especially when given the space to do so. Beginner's mind means letting go of everything you think you know about the person and seeing them as though you have never met them before.

In talking of trust and beginner's mind, I am not suggesting being naïve. Effective leadership is obviously based on a lot of experience and requires a degree of wisdom. We have to make difficult decisions at times. This expertise is not lost with beginner's mind. In fact, we can't lose the expertise we have acquired; it will naturally surface in our mind when we need it. In this sense, we don't need to concern ourselves too much with it and certainly not use like a pair of sunglasses to filter what we see. One of the key features of wisdom is receptivity – the ability to be open to situations and respond in a creative way. It is not something that is set in stone – quite the opposite. Seeing things more openly in this way will actually help pick up on problems. When we make mistakes, it is often because we are so fixed on our own agenda that we fail to notice subtle signs that something is not quite right. One expression of this openness is trusting others. The building of trust is a reciprocal one: one person reveals something about themselves, which leads to the other person do the same, the first person responds to this and so on. Trust builds trust, which in turn builds goodwill, which makes positive things happen.

It is a basic organisational principle that areas with a particular function can be usefully grouped into a single unit. This helps to focus both planning and operation and is the reason we have departments, companies, teams and so on. For similar reasons, organisations themselves are focussed on one or more functions, sets of products or services. Useful though this is, it can play into our evolutionary tendencies to become tribal. Again, this need not be a problem but if it becomes entrenched it can lead to lost opportunities. It is always useful to look outwards from the team as a balance to looking at the team itself.

I once saw a training video about communication which caricatured a figure who had the attitude of "don't interrupt when I'm working" and hid behind a stack of books to try and put off people approaching his desk. That's obviously the opposite of what we're talking about here. All the same, there is a limit to how much to talk. There can come a point where the talk takes away from actually getting down to do the work – or certain types of work. It can be a fine balance. On the one hand, you need to make a judgement that a dialogue is going nowhere and that your time can be used in better ways. On the other hand, you never know where a conversation is going to go, and there may be something useful that suddenly arises. As a general rule, it is probably better to err on the side of more talking rather than less. There are many jobs, such as sales, where talking is key. As the pace of change becomes faster and faster, so the need for creative ways forward become stronger, and conversations are a good way of giving birth to new ideas.

Chapter 6

Ownership

My first job as a manager was in a rehabilitation unit for people who had severe behaviour problems, such as aggression and sexually inappropriate behaviour as a result of a brain injury. Fortunately, the great majority of brain injured people don't have this level of problem but this unit took the most severe cases in Scotland. It was quite a challenging place to work and the staff were generally excellent. When I started, there was a locked time-out room in the unit where people were placed when they misbehaved. This felt like a punishment for people who were, after all, disabled and I felt uncomfortable about it. There had previously been attempts to introduce a new, more positive rehabilitation system that did not involve the use of a time-out room but this had met with fierce resistance from the staff. When I listened to their views I found they were concerned for the safety of both the patients and themselves and felt that the time-out room was being taken away without a clear alternative being put in its place. We talked about it and they came up with a number of ideas about how to implement it that had not occurred to me. I agreed that they would organise safety training for staff and I invited them to join me in undergoing the training in the new positive approach to therapy. It began to feel like we were collaborating on a joint project rather than new ideas being imposed. After this, it was relatively straightforward to move to the new system [15].

This illustrates the importance of everyone on the team feeling a sense of ownership of what is happening. People need to be on board with developments, otherwise, they can feel like passengers on someone else's journey – that of the leader. More than that, team members often have an understanding of the work, as a result of doing it day by day, that a leader doesn't. They have their own form of expertise which is essential to, and complements, that of the leader. The reason staff at the rehabilitation unit were initially resistant to the new ideas was because they thought that some important concerns were not being listened to and therefore overlooked, and they were right. If we had pressed ahead without taking these into account there would have been significant problems.

One of the things a new leader likes to do is make changes. This may be the result of already knowing the organisation – perhaps having worked in it in a more junior capacity, or from experience with another employer, or maybe having new ideas that persuaded the interviewers to employ them for the job. This is good and often necessary but sometimes it seems like leaders are making the changes simply in order to stamp their mark. A sign of this is the staff feeling demoralised or threatened. I think the best thing for a leader to do when first in post is very little! Initially, they need to get to know the people they are working with, and vice versa, in order to build up trust. Once this is established, the staff will be more willing to participate in new developments. Secondly, finding time to understand how things work is important, as talked about in Chapter 2. The ideas you have may be very good ones but the key to their success lies in the detail of how they are implemented in the specific setting you work in. It is not enough to frame your ideas in such a way that the workforce can more easily accept them. It is better if the ideas are actually created in collaboration with them. This is where you identify an issue and then meet up with the team to identify a way forward. In fact, you can take it a step further and let the workforce identify the issues and call the meeting. Your role then becomes one of facilitator, contributing the insights you have gained through experience. You may well end up guiding the discussion because people will listen but this will be more because they respect your experience than you driving the agenda. Problems of staff motivation largely disappear in this scenario because the team are putting into operation ideas they feel enthusiastic about.

Where does this leave the ideas you have had for taking the organisation forward? What I have said in the last paragraph can sound like giving up responsibility and perhaps even losing direction. I would suggest that your ideas are essentially an offering to the organisation. If we offer something, it becomes like a present. We give a present freely without the expectation of a payback and once it has been given, we don't concern ourselves too much with what the person does with it. Your ideas can be seen in that light. If they are good ideas – and the team/organisation trusts you – the ideas will be taken on and perhaps even championed by others. This is more likely to happen if they are framed in such a way as they are a suggestion. Let's say I work for you and you have some ideas about how I might do my work more efficiently. If you sat down with me and said, "I'm wondering if I can help with your job, I've got a few ideas you might find interesting", I'd probably feel curious and slightly pleased that you were offering them for my consideration before telling me them. If we discussed them together and I felt I had made a significant contribution to the final work plan, I would probably feel a passion for implementing it. If, however, you said "I'd like you to change the way you work" I am likely to feel threatened – am I not doing my job properly? Do you want me to work harder? You might explain it carefully to me and give good reasons why I should work in this way, in which case I would probably accept it. Nonetheless, I would most likely have a slightly passive approach to doing the work and my heart would not be in it as much as if I felt ownership of it. As with motivation, ownership is not something that I am given by you. It is something that naturally comes about in the course of our creating the work plan together. The conversation would not necessarily need to be a long one. It might be we simply sketch out the basic idea together, or that you float an idea with me that I then think about and get back to you with my thoughts. In either case, filling in the details of the work and making it happen will be what gives me the job satisfaction.

It is, of course, usually necessary to follow-up with staff members once they have embarked on a course of work. This can be seen as creating another conversation further down the line and then offering further suggestions. This kind of monitoring does not require individual performance assessment. It is best not to create a culture where the leader becomes seen as the judge of what is good and bad. This can erode staff members' confidence in their own work – they start looking outwards for approval rather than trusting their own sense of what feels right. Individual and collective goals have their use. They can give people a sense of direction, include a time perspective on what is achieved when, and give a sense of achievement when they are fulfilled. If goals are used, they are more effective when devised by the individual or group who will be using them – another example of ownership. I do feel that goals are optional, though. Their advantages seem to be counterbalanced by the pass/fail mentality they can easily create. Motivation is something that comes from within the person rather than being created artificially by goal attainment. That said, some people do seem to find it empowering to work to goals and it is helpful to respect that.

The key tool for developing ownership is collaboration. The relationship between a leader and his/her team is essentially one of working together. The sum knowledge of a team or network is greater than that of any individual, including the leader. The leader's role in this context is to ensure that all the perspectives are heard, so that some available knowledge is not missed. When this happens, a group process takes place, producing an interaction which is greater than the sum of its parts [16]. If a team member has ideas which are clearly at odds with what you feel, the chances are that some other group members will feel the same as you, and if they express this, the process will tend to be self-correcting. In fact, responding to the ideas of this team member is likely to in itself move the conversation forward in a useful direction. In this way, all comments and contributions can have their use.

This is not to advocate a free-for-all, where the leader simply sits back as and lets anything happen. A leader has a responsibility to facilitate, oversee and monitor the direction that the work takes, ensuring that it fits in with the objectives of the organisation. As a leader, you have the final say as to whether the proposed plan is the best one. At the same time, you can also afford to let go of the need to have a tight control of the process. The collective wisdom of the team will often provide the best direction and having too tight a control can have the unintended effect of suppressing views that need to be heard.

It is interesting to reflect that the changes we made at the rehabilitation unit I wrote about at the start of this chapter were not actually my idea. The approach we used originated in the USA for a different type of service and then were adapted by a staff member in our unit and were being discussed when I started there. I was not actually familiar with the approach and had to train in it when I started. It was a steep learning curve for me. I had general skills and experience which were relevant for the post but was unfamiliar with the details of this type of unit. If I had insisted in driving through my own ideas…..well, first I would have had to have some ideas, which would have most likely not been as good as those who had been working within this speciality for some time. This is an illustration of how the leader does not necessarily have to come up with new ideas. There are very few truly new ideas anyway, and many of the most successful organisations have simply repackaged existing ideas and systems in a way which works effectively for them.

Chapter 7

Letting Go of Control

I have spoken about the role of trust between people. In this chapter the focus is on trusting the whole process of setting a direction for the organisation and implementing it. We have seen the importance of a collective approach to planning, and the valuing of staff skills and perspectives. If there is commitment and good morale in the workforce, the leader can afford to have a light hold on the strategic direction. It is essential to keep an eye on outcomes, and these can be fed back to the team to highlight progress, but day-to-day it is probably best to let the staff get on with the work, interfering little other than to provide support and encouragement.

There is a limit to how much we can predict the future. Chaos theory tells us that everything affects everything else [17], and this is very evident in many complex work environments. This does not mean we have to surrender to anarchy but it does suggest another reason for relaxing attempts to control the future. Many traditional cultures recognise the usefulness of being lost. To be lost is to be at a place where previous methods of finding the way are no longer working. This is a call to find new ways of moving forward. The act of being lost requires us to let go of previous beliefs and this creates a space in which new ideas can arise. What often happens in this situation is that we start to look around us in a new way. We might re-look at the information we have, or talk to people we have not spoken to for a while, or simply create some space to reflect on the situation. In doing this our understanding can deepen and we can gain new insights into the situation.

The opposite of this is what is called "bending the map" in the literature on survival in the wild [18]. This is when a person becomes so convinced that they know a terrain that, when they look at a map, they don't see what is actually there but only what they expect to see.

Interestingly, this tends to happen when a person is lost. We expect – or want – things to go in a certain way. When things happen that do not fit in with this, it is tempting not to "see" them or to regard them as irrelevant.

It is based on the temptation to keep doing what previously has not worked – what has led us to become lost in the first place – because it is familiar. Or perhaps these old ideas were useful and enabled us to get to where we are now, but conditions have changed so they now no longer apply. It can feel easier to keep doing these old actions because they are comfortable rather than experience the discomfort of being lost. The remedy is to let go of the old ways of looking at things without rushing to replace them with new ones. If you look at it patiently, with an open mind, an effective way forward will most likely present itself. It may be quite different from how you previously saw things. Given space, the unconscious mind is a good source of creativity.

To allow yourself to be lost can enable a learning cycle to take place. Firstly, the team or organisation works in a particular direction. This produces results but then a difficulty arises, for example, the results start becoming poorer. This is the place of being lost, which causes a period of reflection. From this reflection, new ways of doing things arise which are then put into action, creating the new direction which restarts the learning cycle. It is not essential to be lost for this to happen. The learning cycle can be programmed in from the start by having regular reviews. There is a balance to be made, however. If things are going well, it is best to consider carefully whether change is needed at all. Some organisations equate change with progress but the two are not necessarily the same. Bending the map can go in one of two directions, either denying that there is a problem or seeing a problem when one does not exist. Even where there is a problem, the solution may be to let the situation continue, to see if it resolves itself. Creativity takes many forms including, on occasion, doing nothing, provided this is a conscious and thought-through decision.

The learning cycle points to a separation between reflection and action. This is important. Even taking a pause of a second before doing something in everyday life can improve the quality of what you do and avoid knee-jerk reactions. Reflection leads to insight. Sometimes, though, the insight does not seem to come. This can be because we have a particular picture of how the insight should be. Perhaps we are expecting a big revelation, whereas the insight might be saying "just keep going for a while" or "watch and wait". In any case, there comes a time where it is necessary to take action, and it may be that we feel we don't have as much knowledge as we would like. It may be best to then just act and see what happens. To do something new takes a degree of faith and courage. It also changes the situation, which can make things clearer, allowing us to take a further step.

Another effective way to let go of excessive control is to delegate. There are a number of reasons that a leader may have difficulty delegating. Firstly, they may feel that they can do the job better than anyone else. Given a leader's experience and skills, there may be some truth in this but it comes at a cost. To get caught in the details of a job is to lose sight of the bigger picture, which is where the leader's focus should be. Secondly, they may feel uncomfortable about asking a person who is already busy to do more. Well, it may be that this new work will be more productive than what the person is already doing, or they may themselves be able to delegate some of their existing work. The type of work delegated is often new to the staff member, and most people enjoy a new challenge and perhaps the possibility of learning something which may be good for their career development. To delegate is also to express trust in a person. You are in effect saying "I am trusting you to do this work that previously I thought only I could do". This is an unspoken compliment which will not be lost on them. This should be done in as collaborative a manner as possible, so the person understands your thinking and can contribute their own ideas. Sometimes the extra work may not be particularly welcome, but needs doing anyway, and if they understand the need for it and the desirability of them doing it, they are more likely to be engaged with it. Another reason for delegating is to give the message that there is a limit to what you can do and you need some help. People often have a strong view of leaders. For example, we only have to look at the newspapers to see the negative way in which political leaders are often regarded. Part of this, ironically, is idealising leaders, expecting them to be superhuman and being frustrated when they fail to live up to this. By implicitly acknowledging your limitations through delegating you are giving the message that you are a normal human being. This is actually likely to enhance your role as leader rather than diminish it, as people will see you are being genuine.

Chapter 8

Be a Catalyst

The term catalyst originally came from chemistry. It means a substance that causes two or more other substances to react but does not itself change. One of the key roles of a leader is change. We usually think of change being a journey from one place to another. From one perspective, this is true but if we look more closely we see something else at work. Consider a meeting between yourself and two people working on a project. You discuss the project, make some suggestions, perhaps agree some actions, then go your separate ways. What has happened in the meeting is that things have changed. The two staff members are seeing things differently. You are also seeing things differently. Perhaps it gives you some new ideas about another project, or how the final outcome might look, or it may deepen your understanding of the two people. If you feel frustrated after it, it may cause you to reflect on what has happened and come up with some ways of addressing the situation. The point is that something has happened and things are different. Each meeting and interaction, including emails and telephone calls, has this effect – it changes things. This is another application of "everything affects everything". Ultimately everything you do makes a difference, especially with the influence you have as a leader. What may seem a minor adjustment can become a huge difference in time.

There are a number of implications from this. Firstly, whatever you do may have more effect on people than you realise. A kind word may energise the other person and make them happier, causing them to make a deeper commitment to the work. If we become irritable, they may appear to go along with our ideas at the time but later become resentful or demoralised and demotivated in their work.

A second implication relates to the fact that, in chemistry, the catalyst is unchanged after the reaction. We can say its work is done, at least until the next time it is needed to catalyse a reaction. From this perspective, each interaction we have can be regarded as being complete in itself. This means we can effectively forget about the project until the next time we have to address it in some way, either by meeting up again or setting aside time to plan the next part. Leadership can be regarded as being burdensome but actually, when looking at it in this way, we can let go of things until we need to specifically to deal with them again. This releases us from having to carry a lot around in our heads. It helps to have a good organiser or secretarial system so we can forget things, knowing we will be reminded about them when we need to be. As well as making your life easier, this will ensure that you are able to keep your eyes on the bigger issues rather than being bogged down with a lot of detail. Of course, we are not unchanged by reacting with others – we are affected by them – and in this respect the catalyst analogy does not apply.

So rather than being a journey, we can look at a project as a string of microscopic steps, each one of which changes the nature of the journey. Because of this, the opportunities we have to influence things are almost infinite. Sometimes the catalysing effect we have is to get a project back on track when people have lost focus. This is a change in itself, as it causes the team members to have a clearer sense of what the project is about. They may also gain a greater appreciation of what they are already doing.

Chapter 9

Taking Responsibility

So far, I have spoken about issues such as letting go of control and trust. These are not popularly associated with leadership but I believe they are at the heart of what it means to be an effective leader. Having covered these issues, we now have a foundation for looking look at areas more conventionally associated with being in charge, and a key one of these is having responsibility for your part of the work environment. In fact, all that has been said so far is an aspect of this. People naturally look towards a leader to create the culture of the organisation and by following what is written here the culture will move towards one of kindness, goodwill and productivity. In fact, these can be said to be the most fundamental aspects of taking responsibility, and leading by example is the most powerful form of leadership. This chapter focuses on more specific responsibility issues, particularly with regard to difficult situations.

Where feasible, decisions are best made collectively, drawing together as many people as possible. However, there are times when this is not possible or appropriate. For example, there may be different points of view among the team which do not seem reconcilable or two or more staff members may have difficulty working with each other. In a culture where goodwill predominates, these issues are less likely to arise in the first place, or be more easily resolved. Another situation is selecting staff, where it is obviously important to make clear decisions. But even here, interviews are best run by more than one person so the interviewers can confer. You may be in the position of making the final decision, in which case you can take into account the views of the other interviewers.

One of the key roles of leadership is taking the initiative. By creating space to reflect on a situation, you can see clearer what the issues are and what needs doing. No-one else will have this level of oversight – seeing the bigger picture is a key part of your job. You will therefore be able to consider all aspects of the situation when acting. Part of the picture is the attitudes and perceptions of staff and taking this into account will enable you to act in a way that maximises their commitment. But there are times when action is required that is not supported by everyone. At this point it is best to act quickly, clearly and effectively. Decisions are rarely one hundred per cent clear, so we must do the best we can in the circumstances. In many situations, not acting is harmful, for example, in allowing a situation to continue that is clearly counter-productive. Putting a decision into action changes the situation, enabling us to then reassess it. There is a balance to be made between maintaining stability and being responsive. Often, it is important to maintain a consistent direction when difficulties arise. At other times, it is important to be willing to respond. A "U-turn" can be the most productive decision in some circumstances.

Action can cover a wide spectrum of possibilities. Obviously, it can include strong, resolute, decisions. But is also includes just taking a small step. It might be to call a meeting or run a small pilot project. At other times, the best thing to do might be to wait. Many situations resolve themselves and this can be a good outcome, as useful learning takes place. For example, if there is a strong difference of opinion between staff members, they may both come to you to talk about the situation. These conversations in themselves may change the view of the two people and they may then be able to compromise. They would learn from this how to compromise and incorporate someone else's view into their ideas. If, however, you had made an immediate decision in favour of one or other of them, the "loser" might feel humiliated or resentful.

When it is necessary to take a decision that not everyone is happy with, it is worth bearing in mind that the decision isn't personal. Decisions should be made objectively, without fear or favour, based on the totality of the situation. It is worth asking yourself if your personal preference for one person over another is affecting your decision. It is natural to like some people more than others and there is nothing wrong with this this, but it can potentially lead to biases, as somebody we do not like may be able to do a job very well. The best way of avoiding this possibility is to be honest with yourself. By openly acknowledging to yourself that you have these preferences, you minimise the chances of them distorting the decision. Once you have established this, it is easier to explain the basis of the decision. The people who do not like the decision will then understand how it came about and realise that it is not a personal criticism of them.

There have been a number of times when someone working in my department has applied for a upgraded post within the team and an external candidate has been chosen. In these situations, I give the team member feedback as to why they were not successful. Often, this is less about shortcomings of that person than qualities of the external candidate which make them particularly suitable. This is never an easy thing to do but the team member has generally accepted the feedback. One time a team member became really angry with me not long after I had become a manager. On the advice of a colleague, I decided to give a team member a temporary upgrade (which eventually became permanent) without opening it up to application from other internal candidates. Another team member then came into work to find that the post, which he had been wanting for a long time, had been filled without him knowing about it (I had not realised he wanted this post). He was very angry and I think we could have avoided that by at least giving him the chance to apply. We can't always avoid people being angry but we can take steps to make decisions seem fair.

Most jobs have a degree of stress in them and one of the roles of the leader is to help alleviate this. I have been struck by how many conversations I have with staff are to do with an underlying anxiety or problem. Much anxiety is caused by uncertainty e.g. a person being unclear what is expected of them or not knowing if their job is secure, and it is natural that a person will look to their boss for guidance. We can often reduce the stress by listening, taking people's ideas on board, giving information and making clear decisions. Psychologist talk of "containing" anxiety. A person comes to you with what they feel is a difficult problem. By listening and remaining calm you demonstrate both that you have understood the problem and are not overwhelmed by it. So just by your listening, the person has been able to "give" you their problem and, by seeing you take it in your stride, can receive it back realising that it is manageable. This can enable them to come up with their own solution. Of course, you can also give your viewpoint on the problem as well as listen but this is another situation where it is not always best to rush in with an answer.

There is a difference between a wait-and-see approach and avoiding a decision. This is not always easy to distinguish, as things are generally not black-and-white. It is helpful to tune in to what your gut instinct is telling you. We can avoid making a difficult decision because of fear of the consequences but this is not a good basis for acting. Avoiding a decision that needs to be made can, in some instances, create uncertainty and anxiety. Sometimes decisions upset people in the short term but eventually turn out for the best. In fact, I think a good decision helps everyone in the long-term, even those who find it challenging. If they stop and look, those people can usually find something in the situation that is helpful i.e. that they can learn from. At other times, we may look back and feel that our decision was not the best one after all. Actually, it can often be better to think of decisions simply in terms of cause-and-effect rather than right or wrong. All decisions have an element of faith in them as we cannot know all the consequences of a decision. Also, most decisions have both good and bad consequences. So, rather than thinking if the decision was good or bad, it is more helpful simply to see what happens following the decision and take the next step accordingly. Sometimes this may involve apologising to someone who has been harmed by a decision.

One of the aspects of performance management that is often regarded as key is systematic assessment of individuals, for example, through an annual appraisal meeting. These are generally structured interviews where a person's strengths and weaknesses are discussed and goals decided. Many staff find this approach bureaucratic and approach it with some trepidation. It can create a culture where people judge themselves by some external standard of what they are doing rather than focusing on their own sense of what needs changing. This inner sense is generally more accurate as it can take into account all the complexities and subtleties of a situation in a way that no ready-made assessment can. The appraisal aims to give the person encouragement and address problems but this is something that is best done in an ongoing way. Aim for a relationship with team members that is open and trusting enough that you can both give them appreciation on a regular basis and also address problems as they arise, rather than waiting for the appraisal meeting. The other side of this open relationship is that they can give you appreciation and constructive criticism. This can provide valuable information about the effects of your actions. It is best to meet individually with key team members on a regular basis (e.g. monthly) to support them, listen to any concerns they have, give feedback and update them on the bigger picture to enable them to stay on track with their work. A structured assessment does have the advantage of providing a framework to ensure that all aspects of a person's work are covered. If you are not running appraisal meetings it is helpful to have a check list of the different areas so that none of them are overlooked.

As the leader of the team, you have the final say on most matters. It is worth keeping this in the back of your mind although I have not emphasised this in the rest of the book. This is a major part of your responsibility, coming from the faith expressed in you by your bosses in employing you (or the fact that you own the business) and the unique view you have of the situation. By following the ideas in this book, you are likely to find that most of the time you can make decisions in harmony with the whole team but there are occasions when overruling people is the best thing to do. The important thing is that any decision is made with a kind motivation – "what's best for everyone?".

Chapter 10

The Role of Strategy

Strategy is another area for which a leader has primary responsibility. It is a method for setting the direction of development of an organisation, describing the actions needed for going in that direction and assessing how successfully the organisation is moving forward. Without it, it is easy to get caught up in day-to-day issues and lose sight of the bigger picture. I once was on a committee, part of whose remit was to implement proposals from central government. In fact, what they did when a new government initiative came was to gather together the work that was already being done locally that was consistent with the initiative, and then report this back to the government. This gave the impression that the initiative was being implemented without anything actually changing! The committee had other useful functions (and maybe I should have spoken up more) but it is a useful lesson in how *not* to do a strategy.

A good way of drawing up a strategy is to answer the following questions. These are based on what has become known as the solution-focused approach [19]:

Question 1: Where would you like the organisation to be in 3-5 years' time? What will it look like to customers/clients and to staff?

We could call this the "vision" question. It focusses in on the essence of what the organisation is trying to do. The first part refers to outcomes. What will success look like generally? The second part involves creating a more specific picture of how you would like things to be. It also considers the effect on other people affected by your work. As part of this, you may want to take time to identify all the groups of people who benefit from, or are affected by, what the organisation does. It is useful to spend time elaborating this picture. This makes it feel like more of a concrete reality and highlights details that are likely to inform the planning and implementation process. It is also useful to summarise the answer to this question in a short, specific sentence or two. This encapsulates the strategy and makes it easier for staff to bear in mind. It may also be useful for communicating to others the essence of the organisation. The 3-5 year time frame is common, as this is generally enough time for the strategy to take effect, but you can adapt this to your own needs.

Question 2: What is already working to achieve this?

A strategy does not come out of nothing but is an extension of existing work. This question is about recognising what the team is already doing that fits with the direction of the strategic vision. To look at this has two advantages. Firstly, it starts the process of on a positive footing by a kind of celebration of what is going right in the organisation, rather than seeing it as a problem. Secondly, it makes implementing the strategy easier because it is making maximum use of existing resources. This does not mean that the strategy needs to end up as just "more of the same" (although consolidation sometimes may be what is needed). The new direction might be quite radical, and to see what is already working towards this may mean looking at the existing work with new eyes. This question comes after the vision question in order to keep the vision as free as possible from existing thinking.

Question 3: What else do you need to do to move in this direction?

This is the stage of action planning – who does what, and when. From question 2, a significant part of this may be more of what is already working. By implication, this may mean less of what isn't working in the direction of the desired change. Using these questions need not involve focusing on problems. If you make positive changes, any problems are likely to fall away because there is no longer any room for them. Solving problems indirectly in this way saves a lot of energy that may otherwise be used in criticising people and the resulting defensiveness and resentment on their part. This makes it one of the quickest ways of overcoming difficulties.

To take an everyday example, supposing I want to stop getting angry with people. When I think of times when I could have become angry but didn't, what did I do instead (i.e. what's already working)? I might realise I just listened more to the other person before saying anything. I then found I understood their situation better and, rather than becoming angry, I was able to help them address their problems. It may also be that once I understood them better I found that the basis of my anger was unjustified as it was based on an incomplete picture. So what I need to do is listen more, and if I do this, the anger is likely to fade naturally over time. In other words, I have solved my problem not by trying to get rid of my anger but by doing something that works (i.e. listening) and makes the anger unnecessary.

It is helpful to remember that the success of the strategy depends on the people doing the work, so a key part of this question is what do they need in order to perform well? Much of this is psychological e.g. support and recognition, and this may be tapped into more by the inclusive way in which the strategy is devised and written rather than being made explicit. There may also be some more concrete resources and help that people need. It probably won't be possible to meet everyone's aspirations but asking what will help is usually appreciated.

Question 4: What will be the signs that you are moving forward?

This question is about measuring outcomes. In general, I believe it is helpful to make outcome measurement as simple as possible. This makes it easier to focus in on the really important changes, which can be lost if the outcome assessments are too complex. The main thing is to concentrate on the big picture. The measures should also be specific enough to measure change clearly. Sometimes, it is not possible to make assessment simple and that is fine, provided it captures the essence of what the changes are about. "The signs you are moving forward" refers to early signs of change as well as longer term outcome. It is helpful to look for even small signs of change, as these can be fed back to the team and encourage further progress.

You may notice I am using the term "direction" rather than "aims and objectives". It is often more useful to define a pathway than to be too specific about where and when points on that pathway are reached. Defining outcomes very specifically means that the team will tend to focus closely on them, potentially losing sight of other options, especially unexpected ones. As I said earlier, every action changes the situation and is a source of learning. It is important to be able to make use of that learning rather than dismiss it as something irrelevant to the overall outcome. In a fast moving world, we need to be creative and responsive. Goal-setting can have a use in defining a clear direction at the outset, almost as part of a the vision statement. If used like this, it is best to be willing to change the goal or even let it quietly fade. This is an approach I used when defining a strategy for the psychology service (see the next chapter). The 3-year goal was "have a zero waiting time" i.e. for people referred to the service to be seen immediately. As the waiting list was long, this was an ambitious goal, which was never fully realised even though waiting times reduced significantly. What it did do was draw attention to the most pressing issue, enabling work to be focused around this rather than other areas.

As well as constructing the strategy with your team, it may be helpful to do some consultation with clients, customers, suppliers etc. to obtain their view of the situation. It is also best if you have done some of your own thinking beforehand. You may want to have a general sense of the direction and some ideas to put forward. Because team members are immersed in the day-to-day work, it is not easy for them to start thinking about strategy from scratch and some guidance can help focus discussions. The contribution they can make is valuable, as they may be able to see issues from a grass roots perspective in ways which had not occurred to you. This does not mean they should always be able to "overrule" you, and you may feel the need to disagree at times. At the other end of the spectrum, the purpose of the strategy discussions is not to get the team to agree to your plans so that they feel like their own! Their contribution needs to be genuine.

By the time you and the team have answered the above questions to your satisfaction, you should be in a position to draw up the strategy. This is a task best done primarily by yourself as leader, circulating the first draft for comments by others. It is generally a written document, a few pages long. It should be relatively simple and clear, focussing in on the key issues. One possibility would be to use versions of the four questions as headings. You will probably want to include the core role of the organisation, current issues, a detailed description of the direction to go in, the signs that will tell you are moving in that direction, both short-term and long-term, an action plan for achieving it and when and how it will be reviewed.

The next step is to consider how to implement the plan. The action plan will specify who does what and when. It is usual to develop an in initial plan covering the first year or six months and also specify more detailed actions over the first few weeks to keep the momentum going. When identifying who will do the tasks it is useful to ask for volunteers. It does not necessarily have to be the ideal person for the task, as the fact that they have made the offer will mean they are likely to have ownership of it and be actively engaged. You may be able to provide supports to help them do it. Sometimes, someone volunteers who you feel is not capable of carrying out the task and it may be best to explain why this is. It isn't always feasible to ask for volunteers and it may be necessary for you to delegate the task.

The strategy is primarily an internal document for the team but you may want to distribute it to other key people and/or circulate a summary more widely. It can be good for others to know the active steps you are taking to move forward.

Reviews typically take place either six monthly or at the end of the first phase of the action plan. Again, a collective review is best although, as leader, you will be considering it yourself more frequently. You will have collected information or data to enable you and your team to evaluate how well the strategy is going. In most cases, the result of the review will be adjustments to the work and general direction. It is rare to change direction completely and one of the strengths of a strategy is to ensure consistency.

Having established a strategic direction, you can then focus on the day-to-day person-centred issues that form the core of this book.

Chapter 11

An Example

This chapter will illustrate this approach in action by giving an example of some work I was involved in that led to significant improvements in the service offered without major expenditure. This is may be very different from your own setting but hopefully it will be helpful in thinking about how to apply the principles to your workplace. It is not being offered as an ideal and I have included some changes I felt the need to make along the way.

One of my jobs was clinical manager of an psychology outpatient service. A key issue for psychological therapists is that the number of people requiring therapy usually exceeds the availability of people to do the work, resulting in waiting lists. One of the waiting lists I inherited was very long – well over 2 years at one point. However, the overall quality of therapy was high and people were usually happy once they did get to see a therapist. Things do not change easily in a public service setting and the waiting list situation was in danger of continuing long-term. It felt important to ask "what are really the issues here?". Ideally, we needed to reduce the waiting list to zero. This seemed to require three changes over a 3-year time span:

Obtaining 3 extra therapists – I had worked this figure out by looking in details at the statistics on the number of people being referred, the number of therapy sessions they were seen, and so on. This staffing increase was never achieved, although just before the start of the strategy we did obtain funding for one new therapist.

Internal streamlining – we set a 16 session limit to therapy (with some flexibility) and introduced a policy to reduce non-attendance and repeated cancellation of appointments. This reduced the number of therapy sessions by over 50%. Therapists recognised that they previously had a tendency to "hang on" to patients before discharging them.

Integrated working – in order to disseminate psychological skills we started working more closely with other agencies who also were providing support for people with psychological needs e.g. the local rape crisis charity.

This was before I fully developed the ideas in this book and at this point I was using a "top-down" approach. The ideas essentially came from me and I subsequently consulted with the team to obtain their agreement. Initially, there were some signs of progress but after a year or so I felt that therapists were rather passive about the strategy, politely going along with it rather than actively committing to it. It was at this point that I decided to try and make the strategy more collective and democratic. We held a series of team meetings and together developed a set of principles which defined a direction whilst leaving space for creativity. Examples of the principles were:

- Enabling users (patients) to have a strong voice in the development of our service.
- Ongoing audit of the service to improve the service and address problems (the audit involved collecting routine data on everyone seen, including their degree of improvement, and analysing this).

Equally importantly, making the process more participative led team members to suggest some useful ideas that had not occurred to me. An example of this was referral meetings. Patients were generally referred to the service by GPs by letter and previously I had myself looked at every new referral letter that came in and then, usually, put the person on the waiting list. The suggestion of a referral meeting was that a small team of therapists would consider each referral letter and decide how best to respond to their needs. At first sight, this seemed less efficient as more staff were involved but, in fact, this led to an improved quality of decision-making. The discussion process led to more options for appropriate treatment being considered and greater creativity in deciding how to meet the needs of each patient more quickly. This reduced the number of people being placed on the individual therapy waiting list by over 50%.

Another example of an idea from the team was joint assessment clinics, where a small number of patients were offered an early assessment by two therapists . This was helpful for people with complex problems where the referral letter was insufficient to make an informed clinical decision. Again, despite the extra staff input, it was cost-effective, as in some cases it proved possible to transfer them to a more suitable service. Previously, the patient would have been seen after being on the waiting list and the therapist would have felt compelled to take them on for a long period of therapy rather than transferring them to another, probably more suitable, service involving a further wait. The joint clinic also provided a setting where therapists could observe each other at work, providing a forum for mutual learning.

Overall, these changes led to a significant reduction in the two areas (north and south) covered by the service, as illustrated in the graph. The reduction was not produced by an increase in staffing, as while we had a 20% increase in staffing (the one new person) over that period, the referral rate also increased by 20%. Although we did not achieve the initial targets of a zero waiting time and 3 new staff, major change was possible within the limits of our situation.

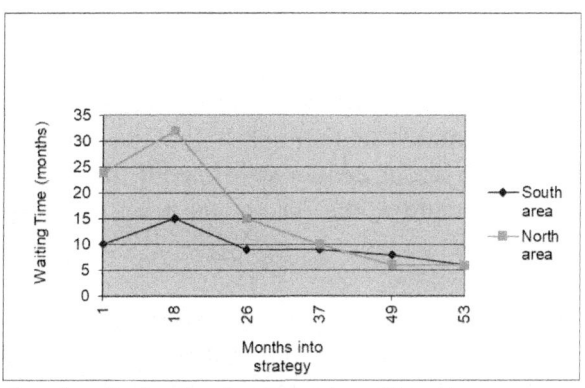

Graph – Reduction in patient waiting times over the course of the strategy

This process illustrates a number of points. Firstly, while the initial "top down" strategy was useful in helping me think more clearly about the needs of the service, it would have been less effective if I had not opened it up to the whole team. Some of the most effective ideas came from other people. Secondly, making the process more collective increased the commitment from the team. By the end, it felt like "our" strategy rather than "mine". Team members were proud of what had been achieved and people outside the team commented on an increased level of team morale. A third point is the need to be willing to change the strategy. After a year, it appeared to be working OK but the signs of passivity within the team were a concern to me. This illustrates another point – that the change is as much about people as results. If the people are committed, the results will tend to follow naturally.

The final point is about my own role as leader. This centred around initiating the strategy and making sure it remained focused. Each time a change was made I considered its potential effect on the overall aim of reducing the waiting list. Sometimes it was not clear what the effect would be, for example, with the referral meeting, and this involved taking a degree of risk by stepping into the unknown. This was effectively a pilot and if it had proved ineffective it might have been necessary to either discontinue or try it in another form, depending on what had been learned. At the same time, my role was a supportive one, facilitating the changes and helping staff gain ownership of the changes. It actually took some time to encourage them to be involved rather than passive, which is not surprising given my initial top-down approach. However, once they became engaged, a momentum was quickly built as they realised their contributions were going to be taken seriously and that I was willing to change in response to what they said. Both these components – active and supportive – felt necessary to me and the balance between them shifted over time, according to my own understanding and the needs of the team, the shift in this case being towards increased support of staff participation.

Chapter 12

Not a Leader?

I said in the Introduction that this book is also aimed at people who do not have a formal leadership position. Much of leadership is about enabling positive change to happen and this is something anyone in the organisation can potentially do. Even people who lead only do so in a specific area and have someone they report to i.e. a boss. Similarly, a person who owns a company, has, in effect, a "boss" in the customers or shareholders who ultimately determine how successful the company is going to be. At the same time, each of us has our own area of responsibility which includes the way we behave. Even a repetitive job has subtle ways it can be performed more or less effectively. There is also the way we interact with our work mates. The emotional atmosphere of an organisation can have a profound effect on its effectiveness and we all contribute to that. Whenever someone engages in backbiting, for example, this has a negative effect which ripples outwards. If, on the other hand, you make a constructive contribution, this can have positive effects beyond those originally intended and also enhance your standing in the organisation.

The principles described in this book – trust, listening, respect for others, and so on – apply to our relationships with our colleagues and bosses as well as the people we lead. It is common for people to be very critical of their boss. Some of this may be realistic but it is worth remembering the level of responsibility a leader has to carry. This was brought home strongly to me when I obtained my first job that involved leading people. Like everyone, I have personal weaknesses and foibles and it became clear that these fed into the way I made decisions affecting other people and became very visible to others. Over time, I learned how to work round these foibles and reduce them. A boss is a human being like any other, and this opens the possibility of us being helpful to him or her, and the organisation as a whole. Because leaders look at the big picture they tend not to see the detail, which is also important. In your position, you will have a unique insight into some aspects of the work. It may be that you can identify a problem that is not being addressed, or that you have an idea for improving things that no-one else seems to have thought of. Firstly, it is important to trust yourself. You may feel you have little to contribute to the bigger picture but your unique perspective is important and, in general, solutions and ideas are welcomed by leaders. This is why, if you have a problem, it is best to go to your boss with a possible solution rather than assuming that he or she will solve the problem. For them, a problem is just another item they will have to add to their list, to be addressed at some point, whereas it is usually more straightforward for them to put into action a solution that someone else proposes. In general, your boss is probably your first port of call with new ideas although you may want to run through them first with one or more colleagues whose views you value. In some instances, a decision-making group or committee may be the place to present your ideas, or your boss might suggest this.

A new idea is often not fully accepted at first, or it may be that people do not disagree with it but it doesn't quite register with them and you get a rather blank response. This is not a reason to give up on the idea. People can sometimes take time to see the merits of an idea or think through its advantages. Repetition is the key here – presenting your ideas in different settings and to different people (it is not usually a good idea to go above your boss in the hierarchy without his/her agreement).

Presenting an new idea can feel like planting a seed and nurturing it and, like a seed, it can take time to develop. This requires a degree of tact and patience but also persistence. If you can quote data supporting your argument or give examples where it has worked in other settings, this is helpful. By presenting your ideas to different groups of people, they may start talking to each other about them, building up a momentum towards it being accepted. It is quite possible that, in this process, other people will contribute ideas that will modify your ideas. This is useful, and is likely to increase the chances of your proposal being put into action. This doesn't mean, however, that you have to go along with all suggestions. It is more about balancing your own sense of what feels right with a recognition that others can make a useful contribution. In effect, you are a catalyst (see chapter 8). Persistence needs to be balanced with tact by thinking how, where and how often to air your proposals. It is possible to overexpose them, which can be a turn-off for others. At times, a casual comment in a conversation can be more useful than a long presentation.

The changes you propose do not necessarily have to be big ones. Even with big ideas, it is often best to start with a small, easily made, changes. If this proves successful, it will help your boss and others trust your judgement and be receptive to bigger ideas you have. It may be that the idea is not your own but a workmate's. If the idea is a good one, your best contribution might be to support that rather than coming up with something different. Again, this helps to create a positive and trusting environment which is ultimately more productive and more fun to be part of.

What if, despite your best efforts, your proposals are not accepted? As I spoke about in Chapter 6, it is useful to see presenting an idea as like giving a present. We offer it to someone but we have no direct control over how they use it. This can help us to not become too possessive about our ideas, even to the extent of allowing other people to take ownership of them – although hopefully they will recognise our contribution. There may be something to be learned from the reason for your ideas not being taken up. By reflecting on them, you may be able to modify your proposal and resubmit it. The fact that an idea is not accepted does not mean it has not been influential. The very act of considering and rejecting your proposal will change the thinking of your boss and others and could lead to them taking a different direction. It is worth looking out for this in the weeks and months following your proposal. Non-acceptance also need not reflect badly on you. The very fact that you have been creative and taken the initiative to present an idea is likely to go down well. Finally, you will have gained something presenting your thoughts, whatever the outcome, for example, experience in organising ideas, presenting them and networking with others. And it may lead to a new idea.

Not all ideas require acceptance from others. There will be ways of functioning in your own job that do not require the agreement of others. There may be changes, perhaps quite small, that result in you doing a job quicker or being more effective or influential. It is helpful to give yourself a bit of space sometimes to reflect on your work and think about new ideas (see also Chapter 2). Don't underestimate the importance of these personal changes. Everything affects everything else and changes in the way we do things will be noticed – at least unconsciously – by others and could influence their behaviour.

Chapter 13

Leadership and Kindness

I have not mentioned the word "kindness" very much throughout this book, even though it is in the title. We all know what kindness is. It is perhaps easier to recognise in others than in ourselves. When we act kindly we are often not aware of it; there is simply a sense of doing what's needed at the time. Kindness is at the foundation of our nature. Evidence of this is that if there is an incident in the street e.g. an old person falls over, people around will instinctively turn towards the person to see if they can help. The people don't think "how can I be kind here?", it is just something hard-wired into us. Similarly, people often remark how much news in the media is negative. If all the news reported was good, we would unconsciously think "this is how things are meant to be – in line with kindness" and not take too much notice. This would not make a profit for the news media.

When we see things are wrong, that same part of us thinks "let me find more about this" with a view to seeing if there is anything we can do to help.

This natural foundation of kindness is one of the reasons I have not mentioned it much in the rest of the book. It can be helpful to cultivate kindness within oneself, for example asking the question, "what is the kindest thing to do here?" On the whole, though, being kind tends to be most effective when it isn't too self-conscious. We can try too hard to be kind, although even that is probably better than being unkind. If we have the *intention* to be kind, it will tend to flow more easily.

An attempt to be kind can highlight things within ourselves that inhibit this response. Anger and fear are two of main ones. Being a leader can involve many situations which are stressful. The stress can be caused by doubts about ourselves and the people we work with. Emotions can be sometimes divided into three components: thoughts, actions and body (or TAB for short, from the initials of the three words). The initial reaction is often a bodily one. For example if we become either afraid or angry, our heartbeat increases. We may become sweaty or physically tense. This is the body gearing up for action (fight or flight). Thoughts may include something like "I'm going to make a mess of this" for fear, or "The cheeky *****!" for anger. Often there is a stream of thoughts like this that keep the feeling going. The more we think about it, the longer the feeling lasts. Thinking can even produce an emotion without any external provocation. For example, worry is a stream of thoughts that on its own can produce anxiety. The third component is how we act on the feeling. Being unaware of the thoughts and bodily sensations can lead to an overreaction, for example, speaking angrily and saying things we later regret, or, giving in to someone when we are afraid, when it would be really best to stand our ground. To break free of this, we need to stand back and look inwards at our own reaction rather than just focusing on the situation in front of us. Take a breath. By recognising that we are afraid, stressed or angry, we bring these emotions into conscious awareness, which means they are no longer controlling us. This creates a space where we can actively choose how best to act. Given this choice, people tend to act more kindly than they otherwise would have done. This means we can act effectively even when we have these feelings . The process I have described here is a form of genuineness, which was covered in Chapter 3. Emotions can be useful and it is not necessary to try to get rid of them, but to see them as part of a bigger picture rather than letting them control our actions.

Kindness can seem like a soft option but it does not stand against clear decision-making. I have seen a fair bit of poor decision-making in the public sector and elsewhere and this is often the result of one of two things. The most common is fear of change. People can be afraid of either offending someone or simply going into the unknown. Hopefully the collaborative approach described in this book will help minimise the number of people who feel alienated by the changes. It is normal to feel challenged by going into the unknown, but with support and involvement people are more likely to see it as an exciting opportunity. The second common cause for poor decision-making is excess personal ambition on the part of the leader. Sometimes a new manager will come into a new post and try to change things quickly in order to prove themselves. The symptoms of this type of change is staff feeling alienated and a sense of "change for the sake of change". Of course, it is rare that everyone will be happy with change but neither should most people feel unhappy.

In contrast, decisions fuelled by kindness tend to be productive. The main thing is to look at the totality of the situation. Kindness needs to apply to everyone, not just the person in front of us or the one who is most vociferous. Often there seems to be a conflict between peoples' needs in a situation but experience has shown me that a good decision ultimately tends to be in the best interests of everyone.

Kindness also takes courage. Trying to be kind in a position of leadership can feel like swimming against the stream. We may feel there is an expectation from others (or even ourselves) to be more authoritarian or "dynamic". The fact that you are reading this book shows that you feel there is something more to leadership than this, and in following this sense you will be moving towards a more fulfilling and effective job for both yourself and those around you.

REFERENCES

1. Health and Safety Executive, UK, *Work related stress depression or anxiety statistics in Great Britain, 2018.*
2. Hunter, P.A., *Breaking the Mould: True Stories About Ordinary People Becoming Powerful* (New Delhi; Sterling, 2007).
3. Dominguez, J. & Robin, V., Your Money or Your Life (New York; Penguin, 1992).
4. Judge, T.A. *et al.*, The relationship between pay and job satisfaction: A meta-analysis of the literature. *Journal of Vocational Behavior.* **77**: 157–167., 2010.
5. Dictionary definitions are taken from the *Chambers Twentieth Century Dictionary* (1972).
6. Buzan, T., *How to Mind Map: The Ultimate Thinking Tool That Will Change Your Life Paperback* (London; Thorsons, 2002)

7. Wiseman, R., *The Luck Factor* (London; Arrow, 2004).
8. Rogers, C., *A Way of Being* (Boston; Houghton Mifflin, 1996).
9. Thaler, L.K. & Koval, R., *The Power of Nice: How to conquer the business world with kindness* (New York; Crown, 2006).
10. Lehrer, J., *Imagine: How creativity works* (Edinburgh; Canongate, 2012).
11. See *The Luck Factor*, op. cit., Chapter 3, Sub-principle 2.
12. Thaler, L.K. & Koval, R., *The Power of Nice: How to conquer the business world with kindness* (New York; Crown, 2006).
13. For example, D'Souza, S., *Brilliant Networking* (Harlow; Prentice-Hall, 2011).
14. Suzuki, S. *Zen Mind, Beginner's Mind* (Boston; Shambala, 2006).
15. Rothwell, N., LaVigna G.W. Willis T.J., A non-aversive rehabilitation approach for people with severe behavioural

problems resulting from brain injury. *Brain Injury.* 1999, **13**: 521-33.
16. Freshley, C., *The Wisdom of Group Decisions* (Brunswick, ME; Good Group Decisions, 2010).
17. Gleick, J., *Chaos: Making a New Science* (New York; Vintage, 1997).
18. Gonsalves, L., *Deep Survival*: Who Lives, Who Dies and Why (New York; Norton, 2005).
19. Lueger, G & Korn, H, (eds.) Solution-Focused Management (Munich; Rainer Hampp, 2006).

Printed in Great Britain
by Amazon